Other Biographies from Tamarind Books

The Life of Stephen Lawrence
Barack Obama: The Making of a President
Michelle Obama: The Making of a First Lady

Malorie Blackman – Author
Benjamin Zephaniah – Poet
Rudolph Walker – Actor
David Grant – Voice Coach
Chinwe Roy – Artist
Samantha Tross – Surgeon

Fiction

Now Is the Time for Running *by Michael Williams*
Camp Gold: Running Stars *by Christine Ohuruogu*
Camp Gold: Going for Gold *by Christine Ohuruogu*
Skin Deep *by Malaika Rose Stanley*
The Young Chieftain *by Ken Howard*

Tamarind Books – See yourselves in our books.
We believe all children should be valued for who they are.
They should live in an environment which respects their own
identity, culture and heritage and they should meet people
like themselves in the books they read.

Visit our website www.**tamarindbooks**.co.uk
Follow us on Twitter @Tamarindbooks

With many thanks to Christine and Patience Ohuruogu,
Elaine Petch, Ross Garritty, and Shah Khan

TAMARIND STARS: SPORTING HEROES
A TAMARIND BOOK 978 1 848 53097 3

First published in Great Britain by Tamarind Books,
an imprint of Random House Children's Publishers UK
A Random House Group Company

Tamarind Books edition published 2012

1 3 5 7 9 10 8 6 4 2

Penguin Random House is committed to a sustainable future for
our business, our readers and our planet. This book is made from
Forest Stewardship Council® certified paper.

MIX
Paper from
responsible sources
FSC® C018179

Printed and bound in Great Britain by Clays Ltd, St Ives plc

Set in Humanist

Tamarind Books are published by Random House Children's Publishers UK,
61–63 Uxbridge Road, London W5 5SA

www.kidsatrandomhouse.co.uk
www.totallyrandombooks.co.uk
www.tamarindbooks.co.uk

Addresses for companies within The Random House Group Limited can be
found at: www.randomhouse.co.uk/offices.htm

THE RANDOM HOUSE GROUP Limited Reg. No. 954009

A CIP catalogue record for this book is available from the British Library.

TAMARIND STARS

Sporting Heroes

RUTH REDFORD

TAMARIND

Contents

✦ ✳ ✦

THE MAKING OF A SPORTING HERO

* * *

In the UK there are approximately 15,000 professional sportsmen and women. Those at the top of their chosen sport are often sporting heroes, role models to many. What unites them all? Firstly, it's clear that they all have a great determination to be the best and to win. Secondly, they must be willing to make sacrifices to attain their goal.

Being dedicated to a sport can mean leading quite an unusual life, and many top athletes have to make an extra effort to find ways to fit the rest of their lives around their training. For young sports-people aiming to be the best, it means working out a balance between important school study and training. They often don't have time to have a big social life either: they may have to get up early and spend hours at the training ground both before and after the normal school day. It's not easy!

Younger athletes need to remember to work hard at school or college too, so that they have as many options as possible in the future. Many athletes go into coaching or sports management after their own sporting careers have peaked, and these jobs need good qualifications. While training, young athletes also often need to work part-time, as they usually don't have funding until they are older, and it is easier to find part-time work if you've had a good education.

In this book we are focusing on a few of the sporting heroes who are achieving phenomenal records and have succeeded against difficult odds.

They are an inspiration to us all.

MAJOR SPORTING EVENTS AROUND THE WORLD

SUMMER OLYMPICS

The Summer Olympics is one of the biggest sporting events in the world. Millions visit the host country to watch and support their chosen athletes. Billions around the world follow the competition on television and the internet.

The Summer Olympics . . .
* was started over 2000 years ago
* was revived in 1896
* takes place every four years
* holds more than 300 different events over sixteen days
* hosts around 11,000 top sportsmen and women.

PARALYMPICS

The Paralympics are sporting events for athletes who have a disability of some kind – with the emphasis clearly on athletic achievement rather than on disability. The Paralympic Games are held in the same year as the Olympic Games and the number of competitors goes up each year. When they were first introduced in Rome in 1960, there were 400 athletes in total – at the last Olympics in 2008 there were over 3900!

NATIONAL AND WORLD
SPORTING EVENTS

Every four years people of all countries watch the Olympics with huge excitement. Winter sports – like skiing, snowboarding and ice skating – also have their own Winter Olympics every four years; and, of course, everyone knows of the four-yearly World Cup championships for football. But these are not the only major events for sportsmen and women.

Each section of every sport has its own competitions, and for most sports World Championships and European Championships are held once every two years. Countries also hold their own national events. These are all important to enable sportspeople to showcase their talents and compete against others.

JUNIOR CHAMPIONSHIPS

For young people, almost every sport holds junior championships. Most adult sporting heroes began by working their way up through the juniors in their chosen sport.

CHAPTER ONE

CHRISTINE OHURUOGU

'Everyone dreams about winning.
But you never think it's a reality.'

Christine Ohuruogu has been competing in athletics since she was sixteen years old. An impressive athlete, she won gold in the 400 metres at the Beijing Olympics in 2008 and is part of Team GB's Olympic squad for the London 2012 Olympics. In 2009 she was awarded an MBE in the New Year's Honours list.

CHRISTINE'S FAMILY

Christine was born in Newham, East London, on 17 May 1984 to Igbo Nigerian parents. When Jonathan and Patience Ohuruogu gazed down lovingly at the tiny baby in their arms they had no idea that she was going to be an Olympic gold medallist and a sporting hero!

Christine's dad, Jonathan, used to work as a chief marine engineer, but then became self-employed and worked from home. Her mum, Patience, works for the tax office. Although they both enjoyed sport when they were younger, neither of Christine's parents ever had the opportunities that she has been given through the various clubs and schools that she attended.

Christine's family is a big one. She's the second oldest and has seven brothers and sisters. She's very close to her older brother, Obi, and they used to have great fun together as young children.

Her youngest brother, Joshua, is twenty-four years younger than her! He's a big fan and likes to watch his older sister running. He is always honest with her about how he thinks she has done in her latest race.

Christine could be a mischievous child, although her mother mostly remembers her as a very helpful little girl, who was also serious about her schoolwork. At school, in fact, Christine was a model student. Her father knew that education was important and was very clear about what he expected from his children – all of them. Before Christine started running professionally her parents never realized that athletics could even be a career, let alone that they'd become the proud parents of an Olympic Champion.

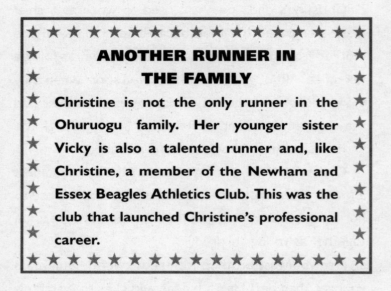

★ ★ ★ ★ ★ ★ ★ ★ ★ ★ ★ ★ ★ ★ ★ ★ ★ ★ ★

ANOTHER RUNNER IN
THE FAMILY

Christine is not the only runner in the Ohuruogu family. Her younger sister Vicky is also a talented runner and, like Christine, a member of the Newham and Essex Beagles Athletics Club. This was the club that launched Christine's professional career.

★ ★ ★ ★ ★ ★ ★ ★ ★ ★ ★ ★ ★ ★ ★ ★ ★ ★ ★

CHRISTINE'S SCHOOLDAYS

Christine loved primary school and remembers playtime as being the best time of the day. After school she was always very active; it didn't matter what sport it was, she just enjoyed being outside – on bikes, rollerskates, skateboards, or just kicking a ball around. Christine played for different sports clubs every weekend – it kept her very busy!

From primary school she went to St Edward's

secondary school in Romford. The school had good sporting facilities and it was there that Christine started to take an interest in netball. She didn't make the team the first time but persevered and was accepted on her second tryout.

AN ALL-ROUNDER!

Christine has played almost all sports. She enjoys hockey, rugby, rounders, tennis, trampolining and basketball. Christine recommends trying lots of sports to find out what works best for you – everybody is different.

When Christine was fifteen years old she ran the 800 metres for the first time – at her school sports day. She was keen to outdo her siblings and wanted to go home with a trophy and she did! Nobody realized that this was only the start of her winning streak.

Christine did well in her GCSEs and went to Woodford Green for her sixth-form studies. By the end of these next two years, she was still studying hard, playing netball for the England Under-17 team and also starting to run more.

Christine gained three A levels – in History, English, Biology – and an AS level in Psychology.

After her A levels, Christine went to University College London, where she studied Linguistics, eventually graduating with a 2.1 degree.

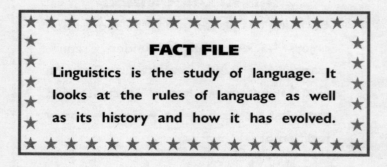

★ ★ ★ ★ ★ ★ ★ ★ ★ ★ ★ ★ ★ ★ ★ ★ ★ ★

FACT FILE

Linguistics is the study of language. It looks at the rules of language as well as its history and how it has evolved.

★ ★ ★ ★ ★ ★ ★ ★ ★ ★ ★ ★ ★ ★ ★ ★ ★ ★

During this time she also competed for the England Under-19 netball team. However, it was running that she was really interested in, and she found herself training harder and running better and better. Finally, after winning a gold medal in the 400 metres at the 2006 Commonwealth Games, she realized that her career path would be in athletics.

CHRISTINE'S ATHLETICS CAREER

At the age of sixteen, Christine joined the Newham and Essex Beagles Athletics Club and her talent for running was instantly recognized. Although she was already playing netball for England she was encouraged to concentrate on athletics. The Newham and Essex Beagles coaches could see straight away that Christine had a remarkable talent. She had no training, but was beating girls who had been running for years. Sometimes she trained with the boys because she was so fast!

★ ★ ★ ★ ★ ★ ★ ★ ★ ★ ★ ★ ★ ★ ★ ★ ★

RUNNING FOR BRITAIN

Christine first raced for Britain when she was seventeen. She hadn't planned on competing, but when a slot became available in the World Championships, she was keen to participate. She came third out of the seven girls running.

When she was nineteen, Christine entered the Junior European Championships.

★ ★ ★ ★ ★ ★ ★ ★ ★ ★ ★ ★ ★ ★ ★ ★ ★

To everyone's surprise she won a bronze medal – an incredible result! It was clear that she had an amazing talent and now she decided to focus solely on athletics and leave the netball behind.

HOW FAST IS FAST ENOUGH?

The current world record holders in the 400 metres are:

* Men's: Michael Johnson, who in 1999 ran it in 43.18 seconds
* Women's: Marita Koch, 47.60 seconds, set in 1985
* The fastest land animal is a cheetah – it can run 400 metres in 12 seconds
* An average human adult can run at speeds of between 13 and 20 m.p.h. This can mean covering 400 metres in around 60 seconds

At the Helsinki World Championships in 2005, Christine was in the 400-metre British team – here she helped the team win a bronze medal in the 4 x 400 metres relay event.

The next year she was entered for the Commonwealth Games. Could she beat the Olympic champion, Tonique Williams-Darling? Not many people thought that she would be able to – but running an impressive home straight, she took gold and achieved a personal best of 50.28 seconds.

BANNED

On the eve of the 2006 World Championships, Christine received a real blow. It was announced that she would be banned from competing for one year for failing to attend three out-of-competition drugs tests. Christine was devastated.

All athletes must take these tests regularly and Christine knew they were very important, but there were good reasons why she had messed up her tests schedule. Sometimes her training routine moved her from one training ground to another at short notice, and it often meant she didn't quite know where she was going to be from one day to the next. On the day of her third test that year, for instance, she missed it because her training that day was based at Crystal Palace instead of being in Mile End. The fact that her Achilles tendon was playing up at this time also contributed to her disorganization.

★ ★ ★ ★ ★ ★ ★ ★ ★ ★ ★ ★ ★ ★ ★ ★ ★ ★

★ **ACHILLES TENDON** ★

★ **The Achilles tendon connects the two** ★

★ **major calf muscles to the back of the heel** ★

★ **bone. When it is overworked it can tighten** ★

★ **and even tear. Athletes must always take** ★

★ **care of this crucial part of their body. When** ★

★ **injured, it needs rest and sometimes an** ★

★ **operation to make it better.** ★

★ ★ ★ ★ ★ ★ ★ ★ ★ ★ ★ ★ ★ ★ ★ ★ ★ ★

When the news of the ban was made public Christine was angry and disappointed, with herself and with the authorities. She considered quitting running, but in the end used the ban time to have an operation on her Achilles and focused on getting her leg better.

She then started to train again, and when the ban was overturned on appeal, Christine was free to compete once more.

WORLD CHAMPIONSHIPS 2007

Christine was named in the British squad for the 2007
World Championships in Osaka. The next five days
were thrilling – her family watched with excitement as
she ran faster and faster throughout the competition.

Christine's times for the 400 metres at Osaka:
*   The heats: 50.46 seconds
*   Semi-final: 50.16 seconds
*   The final: a lifetime best of 49.61 seconds, winning
    gold ahead of the British favourite Nicola Sanders.

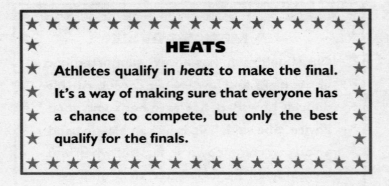

Everyone was thrilled with Christine's result. The decision to include her in the squad had been proved right! There was no doubt now that she was a running star.

TRAINING FOR THE OLYMPICS

Christine was careful not to over-do things in the run-up to the Beijing Olympics in 2008. She ran shorter distances to help improve her sharpness, but steered clear of 400 metres races as she wanted to focus on the coming Games. At this time her season's best for the 400 was 50.80 seconds, and many critics were not sure that she was truly fit. Was she really over the Achilles tendon problem that she had suffered from in 2006?

Christine didn't pay any attention to what these people said; she simply concentrated on training hard and on eating the right sort of food (see page 20 for details of Christine's training diet).

★ ★ ★ ★ ★ ★ ★ ★ ★ ★ ★ ★ ★ ★ ★ ★ ★ ★

SEASON'S BEST

An athlete's *season's best* is the best time run while training and in other competitions in the run-up to the main competition of the season. It is used to give an indication of how the athlete will perform.

A *personal best* (often called a PB) is their best time ever, and athletes usually only count this if the race is run under normal conditions; if there is a strong following wind, for instance, they would discount the time.

★ ★ ★ ★ ★ ★ ★ ★ ★ ★ ★ ★ ★ ★ ★ ★ ★ ★

OLYMPIC GOLD!

When the heats for the Olympics came around, Christine knew that it was time to prove to everyone

– and to herself – that she was the best; it was time to put all her hard training to the test.

In the semi-final, Christine was elated to find that she had set a new season's best of 50.14 seconds. And then, in the final, which was watched by billions of people all over the world, she was neck and neck with the favourite American runner, Sanya Richards. For those watching, it was a tough race, since both women were excellent runners at the top of their form. In the last 80 metres Christine pushed herself to run faster and faster . . .

With a final burst of energy she passed Sanya and won the race!

It was an incredible, life-changing moment. Christine had won gold for Great Britain with a time of 49.62 seconds. It was particularly special as she was the only British athlete to win gold in athletics in Beijing – she was instantly hailed as a champion. The nation took Christine to its heart.

CHRISTINE'S MEDALS AT MAJOR WORLD ATHLETICS EVENTS

3 x GOLD

400 metres, Olympics, Beijing, 2008

400 metres, World Championships, Osaka, 2007

400 metres, Commonwealth Games, Melbourne, 2006

2 x SILVER

400 metres, European Under-23 Championships, Erfurt, 2005

4 x 400 metres relay, European Under-23 Championships, Erfurt, 2005

2 x BRONZE

4 x 400 metres relay, World Championships, Osaka, 2007

4 x 400 metres relay, World Championships, Helsinki, 2005

CHRISTINE'S TRAINING ROUTINE

Christine normally starts training at 9 a.m. and doesn't finish till 2.30 p.m. She does this six days a week!

CHRISTINE'S DIET

This is a typical day's diet:

* Breakfast – porridge
* Breaks – fruit, sandwiches and biscuits
* Drinks – water and energy drinks
* Lunch – pasta or sandwiches to give her long-lasting energy (carbohydrates are important if you burn up a lot of energy on the track)
* Dinner – fish or chicken with salad

P.S. Christine admits to eating a lot of treats – she gets hungry because of the amount of energy she's burning!

ON THE TRACK

When she's home, Christine trains at her local track with other runners and her coach.

She usually begins with a fifteen-minute warm-up jog, and then runs four laps of the circuit. She follows this with three sets of thirty calf-raisers (going up on tiptoes to strengthen her lower legs). This is followed by stretches and then circuit training, which includes sets of twenty press-ups, lunges, sit-ups, split jumps and hops. These exercises are needed to keep her in shape and to get her fitter and faster.

OTHER EXERCISES

Running only uses certain muscle groups, so Christine needs to do other exercises to improve her balance and strengthen her ankles. This means extra weights sessions and exercising in the sandpit with jumps and twists.

LONDON OLYMPICS 2012

The 2012 Olympics are on Christine's home turf – East London, where she grew up. Everyone in her local community is excited at the thought of watching Christine defend the gold medal she won in Beijing. In her mind she's not just another athlete competing in the London Olympics – she's a local girl running for her community and for her family.

KEEPING MOTIVATED

Christine has suffered from injury in the three years following the Beijing Olympics, which has meant that she has had to limit her training and allow time for her body to heal. She doesn't take winning for granted, and the most important thing to her is to be able to compete for her country.

'It maybe would have been a lot easier on my down days to say "Oh, forget it" if the Olympics hadn't been coming to London – but, to be honest, I still think I would have continued. There's a lot more I need to do before I can finally close the lid on the 400 metres.'

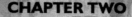

CHAPTER TWO

MO FARAH

*'If it wasn't for my school coach,
I wouldn't be running at all.'*

* ✳ *

Mo Farah is an extraordinary record-breaking track and field athlete who competes in the 5000 and 10,000 metre events, and sometimes in the 3000 metre and 1500 metre races. He came to the UK when he was eight years old and it wasn't until he was at secondary school that his talent for running long distances was picked up by his PE teacher.

MO'S FAMILY

Mo was born in the capital city of Somalia, Mogadishu, on 23 March 1983, to a British Somalian father and a Somalian mother. They lived in a large stone house with several generations of the family. His grandfather worked in a bank, while Mo's father was an IT consultant who lived in the UK – Mo only saw him on his visits to Somalia, and he remembers how his dad once brought him shoes with flashing lights on the soles.

When Mo was eight years old there was a civil war in Somalia, and so Mo, his mother and his two younger brothers came to live with his father in the UK.

SCHOOLDAYS

Mo had never been to school before he arrived in the UK and began going to Oriel Junior School, which was in Hanworth, a suburb in West London with a tough reputation. On Mo's first day he found himself the centre of attention after using one of the only English phrases he knew to the hardest kid in the school. 'C'mon, then' ended up with Mo getting a black eye!

It took him a while to start to catch up on all the schoolwork he had missed. It also wasn't easy learning English at the same time, but he tried hard to do well in class. It was clear to everyone, however, that Mo's favourite subjects were PE and maths. He also loved football.

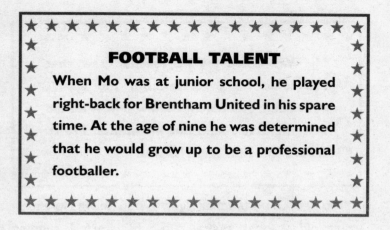

FOOTBALL TALENT

When Mo was at junior school, he played right-back for Brentham United in his spare time. At the age of nine he was determined that he would grow up to be a professional footballer.

When Mo started secondary school his PE teacher, Alan Watkinson, noticed him straight away. Mo showed his speed on the football pitch and could run around for hours without getting tired. Mr Watkinson made a bargain with him to help him train. Mo loved playing football indoors – especially in the winter! – so each time he took part in cross-country training his teacher let him play football in the school gym for thirty minutes as a reward.

A TEACHER'S ADVICE

'You could run for Britain one day.'

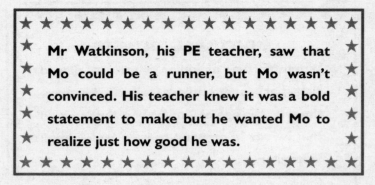

> Mr Watkinson, his **PE** teacher, saw that Mo could be a runner, but Mo wasn't convinced. His teacher knew it was a bold statement to make but he wanted Mo to realize just how good he was.

Mo proved his teacher right. When he was fourteen years old – only a year after he started running competitively – he won five English Schools Championships. When he was sixteen he finished fifth in the Junior race of the European Cross Country Championships.

He was on his way!

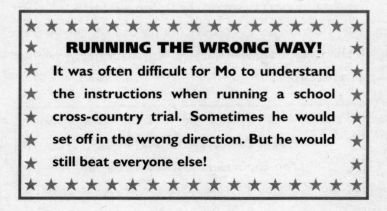

> ## RUNNING THE WRONG WAY!
> It was often difficult for Mo to understand the instructions when running a school cross-country trial. Sometimes he would set off in the wrong direction. But he would still beat everyone else!

Around this time he was lucky enough to be invited to an Olympic training camp in Florida. Mo loved training at the camp and met lots of young athletes like himself. It was here that he realized what he must do, and when he returned to the UK he told Mr Watkinson that he would leave behind his ambition of being a professional footballer. He had a new dream now: to be a professional athlete.

When Mo started focusing on his training, he got better and better. At eighteen, in 2001, he won a gold medal for the European Junior 5000 metres, and gold in the European Junior Cross Country.

LIVING WITH OTHER RUNNERS

Mo worked in a fast food restaurant and a sports shop so he could afford to follow his dream of being a professional athlete. It was a tough schedule! Athletes have to train hard and work hard. When he won a £10,000 National Lottery grant, Mo was elated – he could now run full time.

Further glory followed when, in 2003, at the European Under-23 Championships, Mo won a 5000 metres silver medal and posted a new personal best: 13:38.41 (thirteen minutes, 38.41 seconds).

But it wasn't all smooth running. His career started to stall when a few competitions didn't go his way, and he suffered some frustrating injuries that limited his training and ability to compete.

RUNNING WITH THE KENYANS

At this point Mo's agent, Rick Simms, suggested that he move in and train with other committed runners – Kenyan runners. The Kenyan team were living in Teddington and using it as their base for the European season. They included the world champion Benjamin Limo and Olympic runner Micah Kogo.

Up until this point Mo had been living a fairly normal life, managing to go out with friends and still train the next day. But when he moved in with the Kenyans he discovered a new approach – they lived, breathed and slept running! Mo started to do the same and hit a new form.

He had finally discovered the training routine that would make him a champion.

```
★ ★ ★ ★ ★ ★ ★ ★ ★ ★ ★ ★ ★ ★ ★ ★ ★ ★
```

A NEW MENTOR

Paula Radcliffe is a world-class British marathon and cross-country runner. She has always been keen to help young runners like Mo and knows from experience that it isn't always easy to get the funding for everything. Paula paid for Mo to have driving lessons so that he could drive himself to the training ground in Windsor. And she cheered him on in the 5000 metres at the 2006 European Championships in Gothenburg!

He didn't let her down. He won the silver medal!

```
★ ★ ★ ★ ★ ★ ★ ★ ★ ★ ★ ★ ★ ★ ★ ★ ★ ★
```

BEIJING OLYMPICS 2008

In 2007 Mo's focus was on qualifying for the 2008 Beijing Olympics. He was very excited and trained hard. But by the time he got there, Mo was feeling the strain: he had over-trained – he felt flat and tired, and when it came to running in the heats to reach the final of the 5000 metres, he just wasn't able to push himself enough. He came sixth in his heat and was out of the competition.

Mo was devastated.

To get over the heartache of losing out on such a big dream, he spent much of the winter of 2008 training with the world's top Africans in Ethiopia and Kenya. He was at the Kaptagat training camp in Kenya for two months.

When he left, he raced in the European Cross Country Championships and won silver! His training had paid off!

★ ★ ★ ★ ★ ★ ★ ★ ★ ★ ★ ★ ★ ★ ★ ★ ★ ★

MOUNTAIN RUNNING

Runners train at high altitudes to help improve their performance and endurance. Kaptagat training camp lies at nearly 2500 metres above sea level. That's very high up!

As a comparison, Ben Nevis, the highest mountain in the UK, is a mere 1344 metres high.

★ ★ ★ ★ ★ ★ ★ ★ ★ ★ ★ ★ ★ ★ ★ ★ ★ ★

LONG-DISTANCE EVENTS

If you are interested in distance running, these are the most common distance events.

3000 METRES

The 3000 metres, often known as the 3K, is a popular event for amateur and professional athletes. It is no longer raced at World Championship or Olympic level.

The men's world record is 7:20.67 (seven minutes, 20.67 seconds), set by Daniel Komen of Kenya in 1996.

The women's world record is 8:06.11 (eight minutes, 06.11 seconds), set by Wang Junxia of China in 1993.

5000 METRES

To run in the 5000 metres you need to have great tactics and top aerobic conditioning. To train, athletes often run up to 120 miles a week (that's the equivalent of running from London to Brighton and back).

The men's world record of 12:37.35 (twelve minutes, 37.35 seconds) was set by Kenenisa Bekele of Ethiopia in Hengelo, The Netherlands, on 31 May 2004.

The women's world record is 14:11.15 (14 minutes, 11.15 seconds) and was set by Tirunesh Dibaba of Ethiopia in Oslo, Norway, on 6 June 2008.

10,000 METRES

The 10,000 metres is the longest standard track event. To be a 10K runner, athletes must have exceptional aerobic endurance (which means they shouldn't tire easily).

The world track record for men is held by Kenenisa Bekele of Ethiopia; his 26:17.53 (twenty-six minutes, 17.53 seconds) was achieved in Brussels, Belgium, on 26 August 2005.

The women's world track 10,000 metres record of 29:31.78 (twenty-nine minutes, 31.78 seconds) is held by Wang Junxia of China; it was set on 8 September 1993.

LOOKING FORWARD TO 2012

Mo married his longtime partner, Tania Nell, in Richmond, London, in April 2010. In 2011 he, Tania and their young daughter moved to Portland, Oregon, USA, to be coached by Alberto Salazar, who has transformed American endurance running. It meant leaving the UK, but Mo believed that it would help his running immeasurably and he was determined to do his best for his country at the Games.

In 2012 Mo will be running in the heats for the Olympics again.

TRAINING TECHNOLOGY

Mo's coach, Salazar, uses many different methods to train his runners. These include anti-gravity treadmills, underwater treadmills and a cryosauna – a sauna that is freezing rather than hot!

The new training regime seems to have given Mo a great boost. He has been running 5000 and 10,000 metres in fantastic times and setting new records!

★ ★ ★ ★ ★ ★ ★ ★ ★ ★ ★ ★ ★ ★ ★ ★ ★ ★

PERSONAL BESTS AND RECORDS

Here are some of Mo's personal bests and amazing record-breaking runs.

OUTDOOR TRACK EVENTS

* **3000 metres: 7:38.15 in August 2006, Zagreb**
* **5000 metres: 12:53.11 in July 2001, Monaco. With this time Mo broke the British record for the distance!**
* **10,000 metres: 26:46.57 in June 2011, Eugene. A new British and European record.**

★ ★ ★ ★ ★ ★ ★ ★ ★ ★ ★ ★ ★ ★ ★ ★ ★ ★

INDOOR TRACK EVENTS

* 1500 metres: 3:40.57 in February 2009, Sheffield
* 3000 metres: 7:34.47 in February 2009, Birmingham. A new British record!

ROAD EVENTS

* The Half Marathon (13 miles): 1:00.23 in March 2011, New York. Mo was first over the finishing line for this event!

MO'S MAJOR MEDALS

8 x GOLD

* 5000 metres, World Championships, 2011
* Half Marathon, New York 2011
* 3000 metres, European Indoor Champion-ships, 2011
* 5000 metres, European Track & Field Championships, 2010
* 10,000 metres, European Track & Field Championships, 2010

* 3000 metres, European Indoor Championships, 2009
* European Cross Country Championships,
  2006
* 5000 metres, European Junior Championships, 2001

6 x SILVER

* 10,000 metres, World Championships, 2011
* European Cross Country Championships,
  2009
* European Cross Country Championships,
  2008
* 5000 metres, European Track and Field
  Championships, 2006
* 5000 metres, European Under-23
  Championships, 2003

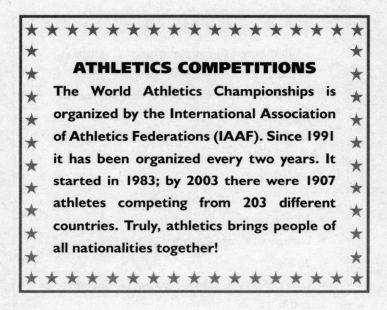

ATHLETICS COMPETITIONS

The World Athletics Championships is organized by the International Association of Athletics Federations (IAAF). Since 1991 it has been organized every two years. It started in 1983; by 2003 there were 1907 athletes competing from 203 different countries. Truly, athletics brings people of all nationalities together!

'Running is something I love so I just keep working hard to do the best I can.'

MO'S DAILY SCHEDULE

TIMES	ROUTINE
7 a.m.	Wake up and eat porridge or toast for breakfast with his daughter
8.30 to 10.30 a.m	Training is normally three or four times a week with his coach, or at the Nike centre with other runners; gym twice a week for training with weights
1.30 p.m.	Lunch is normally a tuna or chicken sandwich; sometimes Mo also sees a sports psychologist or has a massage
2.30 to 5.00 p.m.	Relaxation time, including time spent with his daughter
5.00 p.m.	Run
6 p.m.	Shower
6.45 p.m.	Dinner is normally chicken, fish, potatoes and veg, or maybe pasta
8 p.m.	Relax at home. Mo drinks no alcohol, though, as it dehydrates you, which isn't good if you are a runner
9.30 p.m.	Early bedtime!

ARE YOU THINKING ABOUT GETTING INTO ATHLETICS LIKE MO DID?

* Join a running club, either at your school or at an athletics club
* Make sure you have the right footwear. You can go to specialist sports shops where staff will watch you running on a treadmill and advise you which shoes to buy. It really is important as the right shoes will support your feet and ankles and help you avoid injuries
* Look out for sports clothes made of fabrics that will keep you cool in the summer and warm in the winter
* Make sure you warm up before running and cool down afterwards
* Set yourself goals with your PE teacher or friend – something that is realistic
* Drink plenty of water – athletes need to be hydrated at all times

MO'S TOP TRAINING TIPS

* Don't think of the training as hard work
* Don't focus on the long distance
* Enjoy running – it should be fun!

* Get in as many miles as you can, but don't worry if you can't do as many as you want to

* Feed your muscles and allow them enough recovery time. Lots of protein, such as grilled chicken, is good, and before a big run pasta is the sort of fuel you will need

* Make sure you vary your workout and attend to all your muscle groups

* Keep motivated during training by reminding yourself of how far you've come

* Tell your family and friends about what you're doing so that they can support and encourage you – you'll need it!

CHAPTER THREE

OTHER ATHLETICS STARS TO WATCH OUT FOR

'Never let bad days get on top of you, as a good one is just around the corner' Jessica Ennis

* ✳ *

Both Christine and Mo have proved themselves true champions and gold medal-winners. But there are other stars also coming up; young people training hard and hoping to become the champions of the future.

Here are just a few of them . . .

JESSICA ENNIS – HEPTATHLETE AND PENTATHLETE

Born in 1986 to a Jamaican-born father and English mother, Jessica grew up in Sheffield. She started her career at the age of twelve when she was taken by her parents to an athletics event (Aviva Startrack) and she performed well. It was here that she met her coach, Toni Minichiello.

After graduating from Sheffield University with a degree in Psychology, Jessica became a professional athlete.

Jessica trains six days a week and is determined to be the best. Her results so far are impressive. In 2009, at the age of twenty-three, she became the World Heptathlon Champion, and the following year she was the World Indoor Pentathlon Champion.

★ ★ ★ ★ ★ ★ ★ ★ ★ ★ ★ ★ ★ ★ ★ ★ ★ ★

THE PENTATHLON AND HEPTATHLON

The Olympic pentathlon event for women included five different events and was replaced in 1984 by the heptathlon, which has seven.

★ ★ ★ ★ ★ ★ ★ ★ ★ ★ ★ ★ ★ ★ ★ ★ ★ ★

The pentathlon, however, is still hotly contested at junior level and is composed of a series of events that test strength, speed and agility:

* 100 metres hurdles
* Long jump
* Shot put
* High jump
* 800 metres

The heptathlon includes an extra two events:

* Javelin
* 200 metres sprint

Both events are held at national and world level; heptathlons feature at an Olympic level too. To take part in these events, you need to be fast, in shape, strong and, above all, mentally tough.

PHILLIPS IDOWU – TRIPLE JUMPER

Phillips grew up in East London and enjoyed most sports at school, playing in the basketball and American football teams. But his speciality was always athletics. When he was seventeen he won the English Schools Championships triple jump, and then came fourth in the European Junior Championships.

Phillips's results have included two gold medals (Commonwealth Games, 2006, World Championships, 2009) and two silver medals (Olympics, 2008, World Championships, 2011).

LAWRENCE OKOYE – DISCUS

Lawrence was born in Croydon in 1991. Until 2010 he was playing rugby and was offered professional contracts by a number of clubs. Then he saw his friend Zane Duquemin throw a discus and wanted to know more about the sport. Zane put him in touch with John Hillier, a discus coach, who spotted Lawrence's potential immediately.

Lawrence won his first gold medals at the Under-20 UK Championships in 2010 and the European Under-23 Championships in 2011. He now holds the British discus record at 67.63 metres.

Lawrence also studied hard at school. Away from the field, he plans to begin a Law degree at Oxford University in 2013 – he has put the degree on hold so that he can train for the 2012 Olympics.

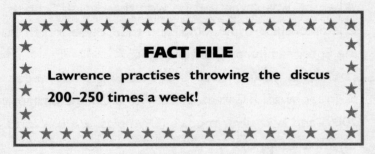

★ ★ ★ ★ ★ ★ ★ ★ ★ ★ ★ ★ ★ ★ ★ ★ ★ ★ ★

FACT FILE

Lawrence practises throwing the discus 200–250 times a week!

★ ★ ★ ★ ★ ★ ★ ★ ★ ★ ★ ★ ★ ★ ★ ★ ★ ★ ★

PERRI SHAKES-DRAYTON – RUNNER

Perri was born in East London in 1988. When she was eleven, a teacher recognized her talent and urged her to start training at the local athletics club. Since then Perri hasn't stopped running and training. She even managed to combine her degree at Brunel University with training full time.

In 2010, at the age of twenty-one, she won two bronze medals at the European Championships. A year later, in the UK trials for the World Athletics Championships, she won both the 400 metres and the 400 metres hurdles.

With a degree in Sports Science under her belt,

Perri is now focusing on her athletics and looking forward to the Olympics. She strongly believes that you get what you put in.

WILLIAM SHARMAN – HURDLER

William was born in 1984 in Nigeria to a British father and a West African mother. He came to live in the UK when he was three years old and grew up in Corby, Northamptonshire. Although he always loved sports, it wasn't until he was fifteen that he discovered his talent for the hurdles. He told his PE teacher that he wanted to represent his school at hurdles and when the teacher finally allowed him to join the team, William proved just how good he was.

It wasn't only sport that caught the young William's attention, though. He achieved Grade 8 piano at the age of sixteen and played the cornet in the BBC Youth Orchestra of the year. He also considered becoming a lawyer.

At the age of twenty-six William came second in the 110 metres hurdles at the 2010 Commonwealth Games. Like most athletes he trains hard, six days a week. He is the fifth fastest British 110 metres hurdler of all time.

CHAPTER FOUR

AMIR KHAN

'You must never give up,
because if you do, it's all over!'

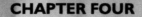

What do you think of when you hear the name Amir Khan? Olympic silver medallist? Fantastic professional boxer? A boy from Bolton? Devout Muslim? British Asian boxer? Any of these would be right, and all of them help to explain one of the greatest sporting heroes Britain has seen for a long time. After winning silver at the 2004 Olympics in Athens, Amir turned professional and now divides his time between the US and his native Bolton.

BOLTON BORN AND BRED

Amir was born to British Pakistani parents in 1985. He didn't have an easy start to life and a couple of weeks after he was born was back in hospital with a chest infection. It was touch and go whether he'd survive, but he pulled through.

With two sisters, one younger brother and lots of cousins, Amir comes from a large family. He says that's why he is so grounded and focused and still the same person he was when he won his silver Olympic medal. People in Bolton have known him all his life and don't treat him like a big star. Amir's faith also helps keep him grounded – he's a committed Muslim and attends mosque regularly.

★ ★ ★ ★ ★ ★ ★ ★ ★ ★ ★ ★ ★ ★ ★ ★ ★ ★

AMIR'S GRANDFATHER

Amir's granddad, Lall Khan, arrived in Bolton in the late sixties. He was determined to make something of himself and provide a good life for his children. His first job was picking potatoes, which was a modest start for a man whose life in Pakistan had been

★ ★ ★ ★ ★ ★ ★ ★ ★ ★ ★ ★ ★ ★ ★ ★ ★ ★

in the military. But he was ambitious for his family and, as soon as he could afford it, he moved them into a better neighbourhood.

Lall's sons all branched out into different successful careers: Amir's father, Shah, had a car repair garage and then a breaker's yard; his uncle Shahid, known to all as Terry, joined the police force; his uncle Tahir, known as Taz, became an IT expert.

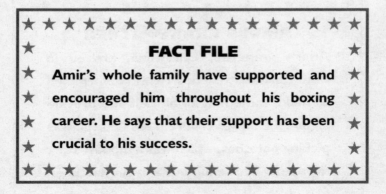

FACT FILE

Amir's whole family have supported and encouraged him throughout his boxing career. He says that their support has been crucial to his success.

AMIR'S SCHOOLDAYS

There was no history of boxing in the Khan family, but it soon became clear that eight-year-old Amir was punching his way around the playground. He was a very active child! The family decided that a boxing gym might be the perfect place for Amir's fighting spirit and natural energy.

Before he started boxing, Amir's teachers really didn't know what to do with him. But once he got into the sport he learned to understand the importance of discipline and hard work, and by the time he went to secondary school he had become a model student. He was also captain of the athletics team.

RUNNING OR BOXING?

At Smithhills School the PE teacher, Mr Dickinson, spotted Amir's athletic prowess. Amir had always run as part of his boxing training, and he was naturally good at it. Soon he was running competitively for the school and began to notch up some success on the track. He won the Greater Manchester titles, both at cross country and at 1500 metres, and was picked for the national trials.

But when the national athletic trials clashed with

a boxing match, Amir had no hesitation in choosing boxing. Boxing always came first! He was talented and was starting to make his name for himself in the world of boxing.

FIRST BOXING EXPERIENCES

Amir remembers when, at eight years old, he walked into Halliwell Boxing Club, which was run by Tommy Battle. The place was run down and stank of stale sweat. But Amir was hooked, and from that time on he started to live for boxing.

As the youngest member of the gym, he wasn't allowed to spar with anyone for at least a year. At that time he was quite a chubby kid, and flat-footed as well. But Tommy Battle stopped that when he put his thumbs under the heels of Amir's boots and warned him not to stand on them. This became the foundation of Amir's footwork – which he's now renowned for.

Halliwell's closed down after about a year and Tommy set up a new gym at Bolton Lads' Club. Children under the age of eleven weren't allowed to box there, so Amir couldn't attend. He took up karate instead, but he kept up with the boxing at home, hitting pads and practising his moves.

FIRST FIGHT

Bolton Lads' Club let Amir join just before his eleventh birthday, and three days afterwards he had his first amateur fight. It was in Stoke-on-Trent against a boy called Mark Jones who was much taller than Amir, but Amir won easily – in three 90 second rounds! He was presented with a trophy.

BOXING RULES

* Each round lasts up to three minutes, and there may be twelve per match
* The winner is the boxer who scores the most points or a knockout
* At the Olympics, boxers are paired off at random and fight in a single elimination tournament. Bouts consist of a total of four rounds, and each round lasts two minutes, with a one-minute interval.

After Amir had won some more fights, then lost some, his dad decided it was time for his son to try a new boxing gym.

Mick Jelley ran Bury ABC and had done so for forty years. He was big, with a huge personality, and knew how he liked things done. He especially liked the boxers to show good manners to each other.

He told Amir that he needed to lose a bit of weight, but that if he listened to him he could become a champion.

With Mick in his corner, Amir went on to win his next seventeen fights. Now boxing was more than a hobby: it was his life. When Amir lost to a lad called Bobby Ward in the final of the Under-13s championship he was really upset. But that loss just sharpened his game and he never lost another amateur fight in England.

COLLEGE DAYS

In 2002, at the age of sixteen, Amir was studying at Bolton Community College for a BTec in sports development. At the time he was planning to enter the amateur boxing event at the 2008 Beijing Olympics. That would have given him six years to develop and get ready, and he would have been able to complete his course, maybe even go on to university. But fate had other plans!

At first no one at the college had any clue that Amir was a successful amateur boxer who had won medals and was hoping to represent Britain at the Olympics. When he told a fellow student that he wanted to win an Olympic medal he was laughed at. He just looked like a chilled-out guy who was very fit and worked hard. But when his name began to appear in the papers his fellow students began to sit up and take notice.

★ ★ ★ ★ ★ ★ ★ ★ ★ ★ ★ ★ ★ ★ ★ ★ ★ ★

★   **A WORKOUT**   ★

★   **When Amir was at Bolton College, he was**   ★

★   **asked on one occasion to give a practical**   ★

★   **coaching session on boxing. He taught the**   ★

★   **students the basics and gave them a**   ★

★   **workout they'd never forget!**   ★

★ ★ ★ ★ ★ ★ ★ ★ ★ ★ ★ ★ ★ ★ ★ ★ ★ ★

THE JUNIOR OLYMPICS

In 2003, the Amateur Boxing Association (ABA) sent Amir to the Junior Olympic Games in America. Amir fought hard and won the Junior gold medal, and an award for being the best boxer! This result would turn out to have a huge effect on Amir's career.

HEADING FOR THE GREEK OLYMPICS

After his success at the Junior Olympics, Amir was asked if he was going to the 2004 Olympics in Athens. The Americans couldn't believe it when Amir said he wouldn't be there. They even offered him the chance to fight for the USA. But for Amir this was unthinkable – he was a British boy, a Bolton lad. Fighting for a country that wasn't his own felt completely wrong.

But it did make him think. And he became con-vinced that he wanted to fight in the 2004 Olympics.

The ABA thought that, at the age of seventeen, he was too young. So Amir set out to change their minds. First he won every competition they sent him to, but the ABA still wouldn't agree. So the Khans had to play their trump card: if Amir couldn't fight for England, then he would fight for Pakistan – his grandfather's country.

Finally the ABA gave way, and Amir was sent to a senior training camp with the England coach, Terry Richards. Terry was very experienced, and had five World Championships, three Commonwealth Games and two Olympics under his belt.

WORLD JUNIOR CHAMPION

The 2004 Junior World Championships were held in Korea, and Amir was desperate to compete there as he knew he'd never have another chance to go. Even though the championships were held every two years, he wasn't sure if he'd still be amateur by the time the next one came around. But the ABA were not keen as they thought the event was too close to the Olympics.

Amir not only got his way but managed to win the title. He was Junior World Champion! And with only three weeks to go to the Olympics . . .

ATHENS 2004

For Amir's first fight in the Olympics he drew the Greek champion, a local hero. But he stopped him easily.

Then came a Bulgarian who was a clear favourite to win – but Amir won again.

His next victory, over a boxer from Korea, took him through to the semi-finals and a guaranteed bronze medal!

The final was between Amir and a very experienced Cuban boxer, Kindelan, an Olympic gold medal winner. Amir fought well, but although he began strongly, the thirty-three-year-old Kindelan began to assert his dominance and eventually won.

Seventeen-year-old Amir had won the silver medal for Britain! Back home everyone reacted as if Amir had won gold! It was the start of a media frenzy that would take some getting used to.

GOING PROFESSIONAL

Amir had always known he'd turn professional but had assumed that it would happen once he'd been to the Beijing Olympics. Now that he'd won silver at the Athens Olympics he had some hard thinking to do.

PROFESSIONAL BOXING

To fight professionally, all boxers must be licensed with a professional boxing association; they fight without protective headgear. Professional boxers are currently not allowed to compete in the Olympics.

BOXING TERMS

Lightweight and Light Welterweight are both categories of weight in pro boxing. There are about 17 different weight sections and three main boxing organizations that offer title fights:

* WBA is the World Boxing Association
* WBO is the World Boxing Organization
* IBF is the International Boxing Federation

FIRST PRO FIGHT

David Bailey was Amir's first pro opponent; expectations were very high as it was a big fight for both of them. But after 109 seconds the ref stopped the fight – Amir had won easily.

Since then, Amir's professional fights have gone well. He rarely loses and he is now at the top of his game. In 2007 he won the Commonwealth Lightweight title. In the Lightweight division he held Commonwealth, WBO Inter-Continental and WBA international titles.

In 2009 Amir moved up to Light Welterweight. Title after title followed, and he held the WBA Super and IBF Light Welterweight titles until late 2011, when he lost to Lance Peterson in the USA. A rematch is already planned!

★ ★ ★ ★ ★ ★ ★ ★ ★ ★ ★ ★ ★ ★ ★ ★ ★ ★

★ BOXING WEIGHTS ★

★ At one time, there were no standard weight ★
★ classes, but for national or world titles it ★
★ became important to establish different ★
★ classes, so that boxers fought opponents of ★
★ a similar weight. ★

★ ★ ★ ★ ★ ★ ★ ★ ★ ★ ★ ★ ★ ★ ★ ★ ★ ★

For professional boxers, the classes vary from the lightest – which is known as Minimumweight, Strawweight or Mini Flyweight, depending on the boxing organization involved, with boxers being as light as 105lb or 47.6kg – to Heavyweight, in which boxers weigh over 200lb (90.7kg), with no upper limit! Imagine a Minimumweight fighting a Heavyweight if there were no weight classes!

AMIR'S TITLE FIGHTS

Date	Opponent	Title
23.07.11	Zab Judah	Retained WBA Super and won IBF World Light Welterweight
16.04.11	Paul McCloskey	Retained WBA World Light Welterweight
15.05.11	Paulie Malignaggi	Retained WBA World Light Welterweight
12.11.10	Marcos Maidana	Retained WBA World Light Welterweight

12.05.09	Dmitry Salita	Retained WBA World Light Welterweight
18.07.09	Andreas Kotelnik	Won WBA World Light Welterweight
14.03.09	Marco Antonio Barrera	Retained WBA International and won vacant WBO Inter-Continental Lightweight
06.12.08	Oisin Fagan	Won vacant WBA International Lightweight
06.09.08	Breidis Prescott	Lost WBO Inter-Continental Lightweight
21.06.08	Michael Gomez	Retained Commonwealth Lightweight
05.04.08	Martin Kristjansen	Won WBO Inter-Continental Lightweight
02.02.08	Gairy St Clair	Retained Commonwealth Lightweight
08.12.07	Graham Earl	Retained Commonwealth Lightweight
06.10.07	Scott Lawton	Retained Commonwealth Lightweight
14.07.07	Willie Limond	Won Commonwealth Lightweight

BOXING BROTHERS

Haroon is Amir's younger brother, but in the London Olympics of 2012 he hopes to beat his older brother's record and go for gold.

THE BROTHER TO BEAT?

Haroon was thirteen years old when Amir won the silver medal in Athens. Amir has even said that he considers Haroon to be the superior fighter and that with the right amount of hard work his younger brother could do even better than he did.

Haroon decided to box for Pakistan after failing to make the England squad for the Commonwealth Games. 'It's every amateur boxer's dream to compete in one of these major tournaments and I was no different,' he admitted. 'I had the opportunity and took it with both hands. I went there to prove England wrong and show them I was good enough to be in that squad. In the end, I was able to win a bronze medal at the tournament, which was something no boxer from England, Scotland, Wales or Ireland managed to do in my weight category. I think that achievement alone showed people I am good enough to be in the England and GB squads.'

OTHER BOXERS TO WATCH OUT FOR

Haroon Khan is not the only up-and-coming young boxer to look out for. Here are a few more potential title-winners:

Khalid Yafai

Khalid was born in Birmingham in 1989 to Yemeni parents. He competed in the 2008 Beijing Olympics but went out in the last sixteen to Cuba's Andry Laffita.

He then won silver in the European Cadet Championships and gold in the World Cadet Championships in 2005.

Since the 2008 Olympics he's started to mix up his training with different disciplines, including swimming. It seems to have worked, since in 2010 he won silver at Flyweight in the European Boxing Championships.

In November 2011, however, he lost out on a place in the 2012 Olympics when he failed to make the weight before a box-off against Andrew Selby for the slot.

Khalid is now training hard for his next ABA fight – and planning another bout with Selby.

WOMEN BOXERS

And it's not only the men who go into the ring. More and more women take up boxing nowadays – and here are two women boxers with huge potential.

Nicola Adams

Nicola was born in Leeds in 1982. She took up Flyweight boxing at the age of twelve. In 2003 she became the English amateur champion and held the title a further three times.

In 2007 she won silver at the European Championships, the first English female to do so.

She won silver at the World Championships in 2008 and again in 2010.

Nicola is now training hard for London 2012.

FIRST-EVER WOMEN'S OLYMPIC BOXING

The London 2012 Olympics will allow women boxers to compete at the Games for the first time.

Natasha Jonas

Natasha was born in Liverpool in 1984. Before she started boxing she played football and karate, and originally took up boxing to lose weight.

In 2007 she won her first Amateur Boxing Association title and then went on to win it another three times.

She then won gold at the European Championships in 2009, and again in 2011.

She is one of seven boxers competing for the three places in the British Olympic team for 2012. She has fought in both Lightweight and the Light Welterweight category.

WANT TO GET INTO BOXING?

First of all, you need to find a good boxing gym with experienced coaches. Try looking on www.abae.co.uk to find your local boxing club.

Some tips for you!

* Work hard on cardiovascular training. Running, skipping and cycling are all good ways to build endurance
* Hit heavy boxing bags and gain power in your punches – a punch needs to come from your whole body
* Build muscle mass. Use weight training, sit-ups, pull-ups, dips and push-ups
* Spar with other boxers in your gym as you need to train with people at or above your skill level
* Try shadowboxing in front of a mirror. To make it work you need to picture an opponent
* Switch your boxing stance. If you can swap your front foot you'll be far more versatile
* Eat healthily, otherwise your good training is for nothing
* When you throw a punch, breathe out; it makes a

difference. If you get punched back and your lungs are full, you're more likely to go down!

* Make sure you wrap your hands to prevent any injuries – wear good gloves
* Give yourself enough recovery time between heavy bag sessions. Train to win! Fight every fight as if it is the last fight of your life.

CHAPTER FIVE

LOUIS SMITH

*'If I do something,
I put 100% into it!'*

* * *

Louis is a gymnast who specializes in the pommel horse. He won the bronze medal in the 2008 Beijing Olympics against incredible odds and is known for his risky, difficult routines. He has been doing gymnastics since he was five years old.

LOUIS'S FAMILY

Louis Smith was born in Peterborough in 1989 to a Jamaican father and a Welsh mother. His brother Leon is three and a half years older and has always been very protective of his younger sibling. Louis's parents separated when he was still young, and his mother – Elaine – took full responsibility for raising her boys.

Elaine's dad died when she was nine months pregnant with Leon, and as a consequence her mother – Louis's nan – became very close to the family. She played a big part in his life as he was growing up and saw him almost every day. When she died in 2009 it was devastating for the family.

The family lived on a council estate in Huntingdon. Money was tight, but Louis's mum and nan provided everything the family needed. Louis was a restless baby, who found it hard to sleep. It wasn't unusual for his mum or nan to sit with him for hours to soothe him.

As a toddler and a small child, he had lots of energy. Elaine would take the two boys to lots of different activities to try and tire them out!

Louis tried football, basketball, choir and ballet before taking up gymnastics – in which he quickly began to shine. The Huntingdon Gymnastics Club, where Louis still occasionally trains, has been his second home since he was five years old! Terry Sharpington, who owns the gym, entered Louis in his first gymnastics competition when he was around six years old. After the competition Terry was so impressed that he said

Louis was going to be the best gymnast England has ever seen.

BALLET LESSONS

Leon and Louis were the only boys in the local ballet class. Leon soon stopped, but Louis continued, not caring that he was the only boy. He used to entertain all the watching parents by showing off, but his ballet teacher always knew who it was and shouted 'Louis!' even if her back was turned!

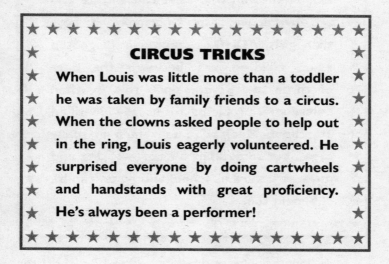

★ ★ ★ ★ ★ ★ ★ ★ ★ ★ ★ ★ ★ ★ ★ ★ ★ ★

CIRCUS TRICKS

When Louis was little more than a toddler he was taken by family friends to a circus. When the clowns asked people to help out in the ring, Louis eagerly volunteered. He surprised everyone by doing cartwheels and handstands with great proficiency. He's always been a performer!

★ ★ ★ ★ ★ ★ ★ ★ ★ ★ ★ ★ ★ ★ ★ ★ ★ ★

LOUIS'S SCHOOLDAYS

Louis went to the local primary school. Until the age of seven he was thought to be a disruptive child as he never seemed to pay any attention and was always getting into trouble. When someone said to Elaine that he might have ADHD she researched the condition and realized that the symptoms matched Louis's behaviour.

FACT FILE ON ADHD

ADHD stands for Attention Deficit Hyper-activity Disorder and describes the behaviour of children who can't concentrate and are overactive. More normally in boys than girls, ADHD is commonly diagnosed when children are between the ages of three and seven, since this is when behavioural problems are usually identified at school. Medication may help in many cases, but sometimes a change of diet and more structure at school and home can be of benefit too.

Louis loved singing and auditioned to be a chorister at a private school when he was seven. He hadn't chosen a song or practised beforehand. Afterwards, when his mum asked him what he had sung, he replied, 'We are climbing Jesus' ladder' – a song they sang in Sunday school.

Louis impressed the choirmaster and he was offered a scholarship, but the school made it clear that he would not be able to do both gymnastics and choir. The choir would have to take priority. However, Louis was already training at the gym most days. His mother spoke to both his primary school headmistress and his coach, but decided to let him choose. The answer wasn't a surprise – Louis couldn't imagine giving up gymnastics!

At secondary school he was very popular and had lots of friends. But his intensive training and competitions got in the way of schoolwork. When his GCSEs came round, he had missed a total of six months of the school year. He took the exams, and achieved five A–C grades – pretty good results considering how much he had missed.

IN TRAINING

Because of Louis's ADHD, his gymnastics teacher at first saw him as a problem child. Although Louis loved the gymnastics, he remembers messing around, pushing people and generally not paying attention. So his coach, Paul, would say, 'Do two hundred circles on the pommel trainer.'

Louis's best event is now the pommel horse – and it's due to all those rounds when he was little!

★ ★ ★ ★ ★ ★ ★ ★ ★ ★ ★ ★ ★ ★ ★ ★ ★ ★

HOW GYMNASTICS CHANGED LOUIS'S LIFE

Without the gymnastics, Louis's story could have been very different. He knows that his training has kept him from going off the rails.

He says: *'Gymnastics is all about discipline. You don't argue back, you line up before the start of a session, you arrive at least ten minutes before the session is due to start, you apologize if you're late. Gymnastics has taught me valuable life lessons; it's taught me the importance of discipline.'*

★ ★ ★ ★ ★ ★ ★ ★ ★ ★ ★ ★ ★ ★ ★ ★ ★ ★

NATIONALS

The Nationals are where young gymnasts from regional clubs compete. Generally the top four gymnasts from each region are picked to represent their club there. Funding for training depends on how well a child performs here. Despite his obvious talent, Louis got no funding until he was twelve – past the age for the Nationals.

Men's gymnastics involves six events:

* Floor
* Pommel horse
* Rings
* Vault
* Parallel bars
* High bar

It's an all-round test of strength, agility, flexibility and power and is very demanding. Louis is lucky in that he has long arms – this gives him an advantage on the pommel.

POMMEL HORSE

The pommel horse was originally a metal frame with a wooden body and a leather cover. Modern pommel horses have a metal frame covered with foam rubber and leather, with plastic handles (or pommels). The event is a legacy from the days when knights in armour would practise mounting a horse.

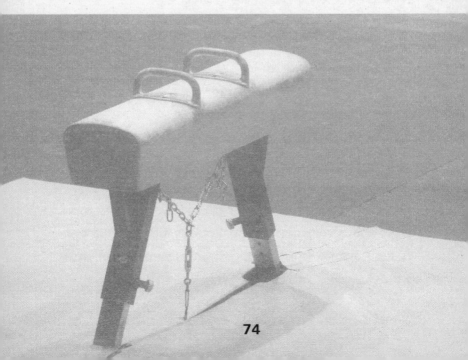

74

TRAINING FOR THE 2008 BEIJING OLYMPICS

Can you guess how much time Louis Smith spent training for the Beijing Olympics?

Answer:

32 hours a week, six days a week, for fifteen years!

This is how hard Louis practised for the Beijing Olympics!

Louis has trained at the same gym for years. In order to keep it going, his coach ran toddler groups at the same time as the gymnasts trained. This chaotic environment was not the easiest place to work as there wasn't a lot of room! But against the odds they managed to put in enough quality training for Louis to qualify for the Olympics.

AN OLYMPIC MEDAL!

In Beijing Louis stayed in the athletes' camp for most of the time he was there. His mum had flown out to watch him, along with the parents of fellow gymnast Daniel Keating. But Louis needed time alone to focus in the run-up to his event.

Can you guess how much time he spent performing on the pommel horse in the individual apparatus event at the Beijing Olympics?

Answer:
100 seconds!

Two fifty-second routines, and then Louis was awarded the bronze medal! This brief amount of time was all he had in which to prove himself after all that hard work and training.

He was the first Briton to win an Olympic medal in individual gymnastics since 1908, and also only the

★ ★ ★ ★ ★ ★ ★ ★ ★ ★ ★ ★ ★ ★ ★ ★ ★ ★
GOLD MEDAL FOR KARAOKE!
When Louis got home to the UK he went on holiday with his friends to Great Yarmouth, where they stayed on a caravan site. They had a great time and sang lots of karaoke. After Louis sang, his friends presented him with his Olympic medal and told him he'd won gold!
★ ★ ★ ★ ★ ★ ★ ★ ★ ★ ★ ★ ★ ★ ★ ★ ★ ★

second black male gymnast to win an Olympic medal. His bronze was the first British Olympic gymnastics medal for eighty years.

Louis remembers being sick with nerves before the event, as it suddenly hit him that he was facing the realization of his dreams. When he won bronze he nearly broke down – he had done it! He had achieved everything he'd ever hoped for!

TOKYO, 2011

At the World Championships in Tokyo in 2011, Louis performed a very difficult routine. Despite struggling with his dismount he still ended up being awarded the bronze medal. It was the hardest routine ever attempted on a senior international stage.

Louis wanted to prove that he could do it and use it as a stepping stone for 2012 – he now had his sights set firmly on the London Olympics.

OLYMPICS IN LONDON 2012

After winning bronze at Beijing in 2008, the pressure is on for Louis to win in London, on his home turf. That's what he's primarily training towards, although he says that he doesn't target medals at European, World or

Olympic level. He just focuses on doing his best in all competitions.

After each major event, Louis has a rest and a chance to go back to normal life for a few weeks, although that normally includes a lot of publicity and photoshoots! Afterwards, when his training schedule starts up again, Louis doesn't do any further publicity; he just trains.

Since he won the bronze in Beijing the funding for British gymnasts has been increased, so now Louis can undertake his training with a lot more specialist care and support. This has made a big difference, but Louis also believes that your mindset and having confidence in your own ability are key factors.

★ ★ ★ ★ ★ ★ ★ ★ ★ ★ ★ ★ ★ ★ ★ ★ ★ ★

TRAINING AND DIET

Louis lets his coach tell him exactly what to do and how much to train and rest – he trusts him to know what's best and how to achieve his goals.

He has fruit for breakfast, makes sure he eats a lot of protein and tries not to have carbohydrates at night. He does have the occasional fast-food treat, though!

★ ★ ★ ★ ★ ★ ★ ★ ★ ★ ★ ★ ★ ★ ★ ★ ★ ★

LOUIS'S MAJOR MEDALS

1 x GOLD

Individual pommel horse, Commonwealth Games, Melbourne, 2006

4 x SILVER

Individual pommel horse, European Men's Championships, Birmingham, 2010

Team event, European Men's Championships, Birmingham, 2010

Individual pommel horse, World Championships, Rotterdam, 2010

Individual pommel horse, European Championships, Milan, 2009

4 x BRONZE

Individual pommel horse, World Championships, Tokyo, 2011

Individual pommel horse, Beijing Olympics, 2008

Individual pommel horse, World Championships, Stuttgart, 2007

Team event, Commonwealth Games, Melbourne, 2006

TOP TIPS

* To become really good you need to train every day
* Upper-body strength is important so weight lifting can help with this
* You need a coach – it's not something you can teach yourself
* Between the ages of five and eleven is the best time to start gymnastics, but you can start later
* Watch as many people perform as possible and learn from them
* Get people to watch you and give you feedback
* Physical qualities needed are strength, flexibility, power and coordination
* Mental qualities needed are motivation, perseverance, courage and a strong desire to succeed
* Remember that it takes time to develop muscles and flexibility
* Try to cut out junk food; eat fruit before a routine for energy

WANT TO GET INTO GYMNASTICS?

There are many different gymnastic disciplines: Men's Artistic, Women's Artistic, Rhythmic Gymnastics, Trampoline Gymnastics, Acrobatic Gymnastics and Tumbling, Disabilities, General Gymnastics and Aerobic Gymnastics.

Many schools teach gymnastics as part of the sports curriculum, but if you're serious about gymnastics you will need to find a club to train at. Have a look at www.british-gymnastics.org

CHAPTER SIX

LUOL DENG

'With each level of success comes greater responsibility to help other people.'

✷ ✷ ✷

Luol is a basketball player for the American team the Chicago Bulls. He moved to the UK from Egypt when he was seven. Later on, as a teenager, he won a basketball scholarship to the US. Luol regularly visits his home in London – where he still has family – and also runs a basketball training camp every summer in the UK.

When Luol goes out in Chicago he is mobbed, so he generally makes sure he's wearing a disguise – although sometimes even that doesn't work. In the UK, however, he isn't such a recognizable figure and he enjoys this, since it means he can live normally, go out to eat, see a movie and meet up with friends. He comes 'home' every summer to see his parents and to watch his beloved Arsenal.

LUOL'S FAMILY

Luol was born in Sudan in 1985. He is the eighth of nine children, with three brothers and five sisters. He doesn't remember his birth country at all – the family left in the middle of a civil war when he was only three years old.

★ ★ ★ ★ ★ ★ ★ ★ ★ ★ ★ ★ ★ ★ ★ ★ ★

FACT FILE

Luol's family is descended from the Dinka tribe and they are some of the tallest people in the world. Luol is six feet nine inches tall (2.05m) and his brother Ajou is six feet eleven inches (2.10m)!

★ ★ ★ ★ ★ ★ ★ ★ ★ ★ ★ ★ ★ ★ ★ ★ ★

Luol's father, Aldo, sent his family to Egypt while he stayed behind in Sudan. He was a government minister and was jailed for three months after the new regime gained control of the country.

Living in Alexandria in Egypt was difficult for the

large family. They lived in a tiny apartment and were missing and worrying about Aldo. They stayed in Egypt for four years and it was here that Luol first picked up a basketball.

His older brothers were keen players and had been taught to play by Manute Bol – a former NBA (National Basketball Association) player and a fellow Dinka tribe member. Luol used to go along to the courts to watch his brothers, and sometimes they would let him join in.

★ ★ ★ ★ ★ ★ ★ ★ ★ ★ ★ ★ ★ ★ ★ ★ ★ ★

MANUTE BOL

At 7 ft 7 inches tall (2.31 metres!), Manute was one of the tallest players ever to play in the NBA. A specialist player in blocking shots, he played for two colleges and four NBA teams. He was also dedicated to raising awareness of the plight of the Sudanese. He died in 2010 from kidney failure, at only forty-seven years old.

★ ★ ★ ★ ★ ★ ★ ★ ★ ★ ★ ★ ★ ★ ★ ★ ★ ★

LONDON

After he was released from jail in Sudan, Luol's father moved to London. Luol's mother then joined her husband there in order to make a case for bringing their family to the UK as refugees. The whole family later moved to Norwood, a suburb of south-east London.

Luol has always felt comfortable and safe in London. Not knowing any English was a problem at first, but he soon learned the language when he went to school, and before long his brothers were teasing him about his new accent.

Although Luol loved playing basketball, football was another passion. He enjoyed watching it – he is a keen supporter of Arsenal – and he was a very talented player too. He was even selected for the England Under-16s team at one point.

But as he started growing taller he realized that basketball would be a better choice for him, and when, in a school game, he slam-dunked the ball for the very first time and made his schoolfriends go crazy, he knew that basketball was the way for him.

AMERICA

Luol moved to America with his sister, Arek, when she won a basketball scholarship to the Blair Academy in New Jersey. He was fourteen years old at the time and his father told him he had to go to look after his sister. But Luol was there to play basketball too!

After his first practice session the coach sat him down and said he'd had no idea how good Luol was. From then on he worked on his basketball as hard as he possibly could. He would wake up at six every morning to get extra practice in before his school lessons started.

Luol's parents were still in the UK, and Luol remembers them always asking how well he was doing academically. School and his grades were important to them. When they visited Luol and his sister in America, they realized just how popular basketball was over there and began to see what a great player he could become.

Luol was ranked as the second best high school basketball player in the USA. The highest ranked was LeBron James, who was so good that he went straight into the NBA from high school.

★ ★ ★ ★ ★ ★ ★ ★ ★ ★ ★ ★ ★ ★ ★ ★ ★

NBA

NBA stands for the National Basketball Association; it is the men's professional basketball league in North America. There are around thirty clubs. The NBA season begins in October and each team plays eighty-two games per season.

★ ★ ★ ★ ★ ★ ★ ★ ★ ★ ★ ★ ★ ★ ★ ★ ★

However, like his parents, Luol always believed that education was important, and he decided to go to college rather than turn professional straight from high school. He chose Duke University in North Carolina.

Duke University had an excellent basketball and

academic record and Luol thrived. He was named Most Outstanding Player of the NCAA Atlanta Regional and he won ACC Rookie of the Week on six occasions. After just a year in college he decided to put himself forward for the NBA draft. He was picked seventh by the Phoenix Suns, who immediately traded him to the Chicago Bulls.

A dream had come true!

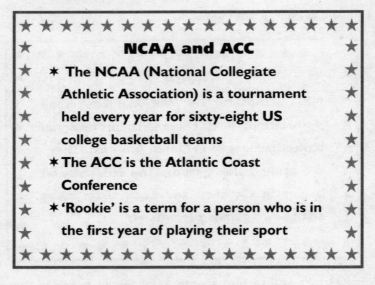

★ ★ ★ ★ ★ ★ ★ ★ ★ ★ ★ ★ ★ ★ ★ ★ ★ ★ ★ ★

NCAA and ACC

★ The NCAA (National Collegiate Athletic Association) is a tournament held every year for sixty-eight US college basketball teams

★ The ACC is the Atlantic Coast Conference

★ 'Rookie' is a term for a person who is in the first year of playing their sport

★ ★ ★ ★ ★ ★ ★ ★ ★ ★ ★ ★ ★ ★ ★ ★ ★ ★ ★ ★

PLAYING FOR THE BULLS

Luol made his debut for the Chicago Bulls in November 2004. He remembers looking around the United Center and thinking, *This is where Michael Jordan, a huge* star, one of the biggest names in the history of the Chicago Bulls, played. Jordan was once described by the NBA as 'the greatest basketball player of all time'. However, Luol immediately felt comfortable playing against the league's big stars, quickly demonstrating why he had been picked for the Bulls.

In 2007 Luol was the only player for the Bulls not to miss a game in the season, and they won their first play-off series since Michael Jordan's retirement. In addition, Luol won the NBA players' prestigious Sportsmanship award for his community and charity work, and they commended his 'ethical behaviour, fair play and integrity' on the court.

★ ★ ★ ★ ★ ★ ★ ★ ★ ★ ★ ★ ★ ★ ★ ★ ★

MEETING OBAMA

Luol was the first sportsperson to be invited to the White House by President Barack Obama, who has said that Luol is his favourite basketball player. He was full of praise when Luol received the United Nations Refugee Agency's humanitarian award.

★ ★ ★ ★ ★ ★ ★ ★ ★ ★ ★ ★ ★ ★ ★ ★ ★

★ ★ ★ ★ ★ ★ ★ ★ ★ ★ ★ ★ ★ ★ ★ ★ ★

$71 MILLION!

2008 brought a new six-year contract with the Bulls for $71 million (around £45,000,000). Being well paid has made Luol's life a lot easier. He supports his family and has an impressive home on the outskirts of Chicago, where he and his friends hang out. He also uses his money for many good causes, including the UK-based Luol Deng Foundation.

★ ★ ★ ★ ★ ★ ★ ★ ★ ★ ★ ★ ★ ★ ★ ★ ★

★ ★ ★ ★ ★ ★ ★ ★ ★ ★ ★ ★ ★ ★ ★ ★ ★

50 DOLLARS A BASKET

In the 2007–2008 season Luol donated $50 for every basket he shot to the United Nation's www.ninemillion.org rescue package for Southern Sudan after devastating floods left the country suffering a major humanitarian disaster. He was shooting twenty-three points in some games so he succeeded in making a lot of money. Over the season, he raised an amazing $31,650.

★ ★ ★ ★ ★ ★ ★ ★ ★ ★ ★ ★ ★ ★ ★ ★ ★

HELPING OTHERS

Luol is committed to raising money and highlighting the plight of refugees, particularly in Southern Sudan. He tirelessly campaigns and raises money in a variety of ways.

In 2006 Luol went with the NBA's 'Basketball without Borders' programme to Africa; then, in 2007, he visited Europe. This initiative promotes the sport of basketball and also gets involved in the community.

In the summer of 2008 Luol returned to Sudan for the first time since he'd left as a child. He was determined to help rebuild the country in any way he could, and, to raise the profile of the Sudanese refugees.

Luol also wants to help young people in the country he grew up in. Every year the Luol Deng Foundation runs a camp in Loughborough for coaching kids. The camp's aim is to transform the lives of children who might otherwise be caught up in drugs, gangs and violence. The Deng family finance the camp and around 260 kids attend.

They concentrate on learning hard work, discipline and commitment – both on and off the basketball court. Luol's brother Ajou and his sister Arek work alongside him at the camp. When they first meet Luol the kids are shy, but as they get to know him, they relax and start to fool around like they've known him for ever.

Luol is keen to run a similar camp in Chicago, and to extend it to Sudan and across Africa. His mission is to reach out to kids and let them know that they can be special and succeed at something.

LOOKING FORWARD TO 2012

Luol plays eighty-two games in a season when he's in the USA. But when he plays for Basketball Team GB in the Olympics, he will only have a handful of games to play. That's a lot of pressure!

Great Britain didn't qualify as one of the twenty-four teams in the last World Championships. In the Olympics only sixteen qualify, but as a host nation they have secured an automatic spot at London 2012.

Basketball Team GB haven't been playing together for as long as many of the other nations, but Luol is confident that they can compete.

It's certainly not about the money! Luol makes around £72 a match when he plays for Great Britain – far less than he makes when playing for the Chicago

Bulls. No, this is something different – it's about chasing the dream of an Olympic medal.

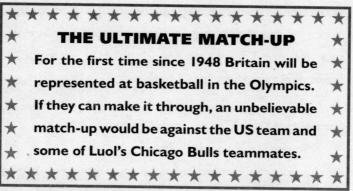

★ ★ ★ ★ ★ ★ ★ ★ ★ ★ ★ ★ ★ ★ ★ ★ ★ ★

THE ULTIMATE MATCH-UP

For the first time since 1948 Britain will be represented at basketball in the Olympics. If they can make it through, an unbelievable match-up would be against the US team and some of Luol's Chicago Bulls teammates.

★ ★ ★ ★ ★ ★ ★ ★ ★ ★ ★ ★ ★ ★ ★ ★ ★ ★

WANT TO GET INTO BASKETBALL?

Join a basketball club, either at your school or at a sports club. You can also set up hoops in an outdoor space or use a public gym or court that has hoops to practise on. Try getting friends to play with you. It's great exercise and a lot of fun!

Some tips!

* Remember it's a team sport
* All you really need to wear are trainers and loose clothing
* Show good sportsmanship. A good way to show respect is to shake hands after the game
* Watch the ball – you always need to know where it is
* Drink plenty of water
* Eat healthily before a game.

The key skills – shoot, dribble and pass

* Use both hands to shoot; one hand acts as a shooting hand, the other as a guiding or support hand
* Bend your elbows at a ninety-degree angle. Push your arm and flick your wrist to give the ball more power

* When going for jump shots, the ball should leave your hands at the peak of your jump
* When you first start dribbling you might have to look at the ball, but once you're better you should be able to move around the court and dribble without looking
* Try using a chest pass – position the ball at chest level and aim to pass to your partner's chest
* Try a bounce pass – bounce the ball to your partner.

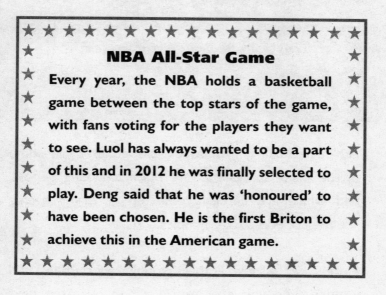

NBA All-Star Game

Every year, the NBA holds a basketball game between the top stars of the game, with fans voting for the players they want to see. Luol has always wanted to be a part of this and in 2012 he was finally selected to play. Deng said that he was 'honoured' to have been chosen. He is the first Briton to achieve this in the American game.

CHAPTER SEVEN

OTHER SPORTING STARS TO WATCH OUT FOR

'Just get up there and go for it'
Shanaze Reade

* ✳ *

Athletics, boxing, gymnastics, basketball – just some of the many sports that are open to young people, and which are fiercely contested at major events like the London 2012 Olympics.

Here are a few other young sportsmen and women who you may see in action over the next few years!

RAJIV OUSEPH – BADMINTON

Rajiv was born in London in 1986 to South Indian parents. He is now the number one singles player in the UK and has been ranked eleventh in the world.

His father has always loved badminton and encouraged his son to play; Rajiv started at the age of nine and has never stopped!

In 2010 Rajiv won a silver medal at the Commonwealth Games in Delhi, then followed this up the following year by winning several European tournaments as well as the US Open.

As long as he remains in the top fifty world rankings, then Rajiv is guaranteed a place at the Olympics in 2012.

SHANAZE READE – BMX

Shanaze was born in Cheshire in 1988 to a Jamaican father and an Irish mother. She began BMX racing when she was ten after buying her first bike for £1.

When she was just seventeen, she developed her incredible stamina and power by racing against male competitors, and in 2006 she won her first professional race at the American Bicycle Association in Arizona.

At the 2007 Track World Championships she won the women's team sprint gold with Victoria Pendleton. She has now won the UCI BMX Championships three times.

★ ★ ★ ★ ★ ★ ★ ★ ★ ★ ★ ★ ★ ★ ★ ★

BROKEN BONES

Injuries are commonplace in BMX racing and Shanaze has broken bones in one foot and an elbow – along with one at the base of her spine!

★ ★ ★ ★ ★ ★ ★ ★ ★ ★ ★ ★ ★ ★ ★ ★

LIZZIE REID – VOLLEYBALL

Lizzie was born in London in 1989 and began playing volleyball at school when she was thirteen years old. When she finished school in Walthamstow she chose to go to college in America and, after success in volleyball at Junior College, was recruited to go to the University of Georgia.

She still calls London home, but Lizzie now spends a large part of her summer training at the English Institute of Sport in Sheffield.

ZOE SMITH – WEIGHTLIFTER

Zoe was born in London in 1994. She began her sporting career as a gymnast and only tried weight-lifting when she was asked to make up the numbers for a team at her gym. Her natural talent was immediately spotted by her coaches.

She was British Junior Champion in 2009, then won the English Senior Championships the following year. Also in 2010, at sixteen, Zoe was the youngest ever British weightlifter to qualify for the Commonwealth Games. And she came home with a bronze medal!

HEATHER WATSON – TENNIS

Heather was born in Guernsey in 1992. She started playing tennis when she was seven years old. At twelve, she left Guernsey to live in the US and began to train hard. In 2008 she won gold at the Commonwealth Games and followed this by winning the US Open Junior title in 2009.

Heather now trains and lives at the Bollettieri Tennis Academy in Florida.

Bibliography

GENERAL

- Sporting Legends by Jill Powell; published by Rising Stars, 2004
- The Knowledge: Flaming Olympics by Michael Coleman; published by Scholastic, 1996
- A Boy from Bolton: Amir Khan by Amir Khan with Kevin Garside; published by Bloomsbury, 2006
- The Greatest British Olympians by Neil Wilson; published by Carlton, 2011
- Great Olympic Moments by Haydn Middleton; published by Heinemann, 2000
- 20th Century Lives: Sporting Heroes by Jane Bingham; published by Wayland, 2009
- Outstanding Olympics by Clive Gifford; published by Oxford University Press, 2007

- Sport by Tim Hammond; published by Dorling Kindersley, 1988
- 21st Century Lives: Sports People by Liz Gogerly; published by Wayland, 2004

CHRISTINE OHURUOGU

- **www.chrissyo.com**
- *Sunday Times* online article by Mat Snow, 11 January 2009
- 'Mirth and melancholy from a dreamer named Ohuruogu' by Donald McRae, *Guardian*, 2 August 2008
- 'Optimistic despite recent troubles' by Simon Turnbull, *Independent*, 24 August 2011
- Athletics Profiles – Christine Ohuruogu, ESPN, 29 July 2011
- 'It doesn't matter whether I'm the face of the Games or not' by Donald McRae, *Guardian*, 25 July 2011
- 'Academy Ambassadors', *UKA*, Jan 2011
- 'My Family Values' by Caroline Rees, *Guardian*, 13 March 2010
- 'Passed/Failed: An education in the life of Olympic gold medallist Christine Ohuruogu' by Jonathan Sale, *Independent*, 25 June 2009

MO FARAH

www.mofarah.com

- Kate Jackson, *Sun*, 8 September 2011
- *Runners World* interview, September 2011
- Maria Fitzpatrick, *Telegraph*, 25 October 2011
- 'Mo Farah's Great American Dream is realized via Africa' by Mihir Bose, 1 March 2011
- 'This much I know' by Emma John, *Observer*, 10 October 2010
- 'I can definitely win a medal at the London Olympics' by Donald McRae, *Guardian*, 10 August 2010
- 'Inspiring tales for London 2012' by Tanya Aldred, *Guardian*, 29 July 2010
- 'Mo Farah relishes golden moment' by Anna Kessel, *Guardian*, 27 July 2010
- Donald McRae, *Guardian*, 17 March 2009
- Interview by Brian Viner, *Independent*, 13 June 2008
- 'My Sport' by Gareth A. Davies, *Telegraph*, 27 February 2007
- 'Mo Farah is the finest male distance runner of his generation', *Spikes* Mag 19 November 2009

JESSICA ENNIS

www.jessicaennis.net

- 'I'm so nervous before competing I could cry' by Matt
  Majendie, **www.thisislondon.co.uk,** 11 August 2011

PHILLIPS IDOWU

www.phillips-idowu-official.com
- 'Three Giant Leaps' by Anna Kessel, *Observer,*
  27 July 2008

LAWRENCE OKOYE

www.lawrenceokoye.com
- 'Games throw Okoye a chance to put rugby on hold'
  by Neil Wilson, 15 July 2011
- 'Team GB Competitors: Lawrence Okoye',
  Telegraph, 20 December 2011
- 'London Olympic Hopefuls: Lawrence Okoye' by
  Saad Noor, *Guardian,* 10 November 2011

PERRI SHAKES-DRAYTON

- 'London Olympic Hopefuls', *Guardian,*
  26 August 2011

WILLIAM SHARMAN

www.williamsharman.com
- 'Hurdler William Sharman – The real-life Gladiator' by
  Lucy Fry, *London Evening Standard,* 12 August 2011

AMIR KHAN

www.amirkhanworld.com

Boxers – **www.gbboxing.org.uk**

- 'When Piers met Amir Khan', *GQ* Magazine, 15 April 2011
- Interview with Amir Khan by Donald McRae, *Guardian*, 29 August 2005

KHALID YAFAI

- 'London Olympic Hopefuls' by Jamie Jackson, *Guardian*, 22 September 2011

NICOLA ADAMS

- 'London Olympic Hopefuls', *Guardian*, 31 March 2011
- 'Nicola Adams aims to be big hit' by Jon Vale, *Guardian*, 14 October 2011

NATASHA JONAS

- 'London Olympic Hopefuls' by Jon Vale, *Guardian*, 13 October 2011

LOUIS SMITH

www.louis-smith-gymnast.com

- 'After a while you learn to switch the pain off' by

Donald McRae, *Guardian*, 3 October 2011

- 'I'm in pain every day' by Richard Rae, *Independent*, 22 September 2011
- Interview by Matt Majendie, *London Evening Standard*, 7 April 2011
- 'Smith stands tall after journey of twists and turns' by Donald McRae, *Guardian*, 14 October 2008
- Interview by Matt Dickinson, *The Times*, 11 October 2008

LUOL DENG

www.luoldeng.com

- *Daily Mail*, 8 June 2011
- Interview with BBC Sport in Chicago, 13 May 2011
- 'Small Talk' by Paolo Bandini, *Guardian*, 5 August 2010
- 'Britain's Secret Superstar' by Donald McRae, *Guardian*, 14 March 2009
- 'Refugee undaunted by comparisons with greats' by Donald McRae, *Guardian*, 18 March 2008
- Interview in *Observer*, 3 April 2005
- Luol Deng TV interviews: include **http://www. blogabull.com/2011/7/26/2294288/part-1-of-luol-deng-interview-about-the-birth-of-southern-sudan-and**

RAJIV OUSEPH

www.rajivouseph.co.uk/

- 'Rajiv Ouseph out to prove he can be a big hitter' by Matt Majendie, *London Evening Standard*, 4 August 2011
- 'Tell us who you are' by Nick Pearce, *Telegraph*, 21 June 2011

SHANAZE READE

www.shanazereadeseries.com

- 2012 Contender, **www.news.bbc.co.uk/sport**, 8 September 2011

LIZZIE REID

- London 2012 Team GB – Profile Outline, *Telegraph*

ZOE SMITH

- 'Zoe Smith wants weightlifting medal', *Daily Mail*, 29 August 2011
- London 2012 Team GB – Profile Outline, *Telegraph*

HEATHER WATSON

www.heatherwatson.co.uk

- 'Heather Watson slips under radar in rise to prominence' by Barney Ronay, *Guardian*, 19 June 2011

Permissions

Every effort has been made to trace copyright holders and to credit quotations and sources accurately; but should there be any errors or omissions, the publishers will be happy to correct subsequent reprints.

Picture credits

With thanks for the permission to reproduce the photos as follows:

Cover images

Getty Images

Inside colour section

i: Christine and Patience Ohuruogu (*Christine as a baby, At school, With her parents, Patience and Jonathan, and brother Joshua on graduation day, Supporting the Olympic bid*)

ii: All photos, Getty images

iii: All photos, Getty images

iv: Shah Khan, Ross Garritty (*Ten-year-old Amir wins the 'Most Promising Boxer' trophy, Amir with his coach Mick Jelley, A fight at Bury Amateur Boxing Club*)

v: All photos, Getty images

vi: Elaine Petch, Louis Smith (*A younger Louis wins gold at his local gym, At school, with his brother Leon, Louis with his mother, Elaine*)

vii: All photos, Getty images

viii: All photos, Getty images